World's Weirdest "True" Ghost Stories

John Beckett

Illustrated by Steve Hayhurst

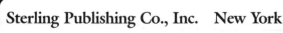

Sterling Publishing Co., Inc.   New York

To Black Jack

The author would like to thank all the people who related these stories; John Fairley, Simon Welfare, and Yorkshire Television for providing the introductions; and Sheila Barry for turning the book into English.

Library of Congress Cataloging-in-Publication Data

The World's weirdest "true" ghost stories / [edited] by John Beckett ;
  illustrated by Steve Hayhurst.
      p.   cm.
  Includes index.
  Summary: Presents thirty-five brief tales of the supernatural, all
of which are purported to be true.
  ISBN 0-8069-8410-4
  1. Ghosts—Juvenile literature.   2. Supernatural—Juvenile
literature. [1. Ghosts.   2. Supernatural.]   I. Beckett, John.
II. Hayhurst, Steve, ill.
BF1461.W67   1991
133.1—dc20   91-15408
                                                          CIP
                                                          AC

10 9 8 7 6 5 4 3 2

First paperback edition published in 1992 by
Sterling Publishing Company, Inc.
387 Park Avenue South, New York, N.Y. 10016
© 1991 by John Beckett
Distributed in Canada by Sterling Publishing
% Canadian Manda Group, P.O. Box 920, Sta-
tion U, Toronto, Ontario, Canada M8Z 5P9
Distributed in Great Britain and Europe by
Cassell PLC, Villiers House, 41/47 Strand,
London WC2N 5JE, England
Distributed in Australia by Capricorn Link Ltd.
P.O. Box 665, Lane Cove, NSW 2066
Manufactured in the United States of America
All rights reserved

Sterling ISBN 0-8069-8410-4 Trade
         ISBN 0-8069-8411-2 Paper

Contents

Warning to the Reader

I suggest you read this book with the lights on.

These may look like ordinary stories, but I watched the people who told them to me. I saw the raw emotion in their eyes—excitement, amazement, and, in some cases, naked fear. I would not want to go through what some of them experienced—something perhaps beyond our normal senses.

There is no need to be frightened—most of these stories are not scary—but they may send a shiver up your spine. You may never again be quite the same person when you have finished reading. The safe thing would be to put the book right back on the shelf. Read it only if you really want to feel that cold tingle at the back of your neck.

Those of a nervous disposition are advised not even to peek inside.

You have been warned!

1. GLIMPSES OF THE PAST

Surveys have shown that more than ten percent of the population claim they have seen ghosts.

But what have they really seen? Dead people coming back to life? Images from their own minds? Or perhaps something like videotapes of reality, played not at the wrong speed, but at the wrong time?

For most of us, time flows inexorably past, like an escalator, or a moving walkway in an airport. We get swept along, and we can't help getting older—even if we never get much wiser! But just occasionally some people seem to stumble on images from another time. They somehow break the rules, and then they may see fragments from the future . . .

. . . or glimpses of the past.

The Vanishing Bookstore

As actress Shirley Lawrence crossed the street from Paramount Studios in Hollywood, she noticed a small bookstore. It was tucked into a large building with a restaurant and offices: 5476 Marathon Avenue. She was surprised, because she had never noticed the bookstore before, but she wandered in off the street, walked down a few steps, and had a look round.

She was browsing at a stack labelled METAPHYSI-CAL BOOKS when the woman at the desk said, "Wait just a minute. I have something that I'm sure will interest you."

She disappeared into the back of the shop, and came back a minute later with a book that she pressed into Shirley's hands—a thick green book, old and faded. "I know you'll enjoy this."

Shirley was puzzled. The book was *Ardath* by Marie Corelli. She had not heard of it. How should she take this curious offer? "Thank you," she said. "How much is it?"

"Oh, there's no charge," the woman said. "I want you to have it, since I know it will appeal to you."

She was right. Shirley did enjoy the book. She was amazed that the woman had known what would interest her, and immediately decided to read other books by Marie Corelli. Since then she has brought nine more.

The next time she left Paramount with a few minutes to spare, Shirley crossed the street again to thank the woman in the bookstore.

She could not find it.

She asked at other shops in the block, but they could not remember ever having seen a bookstore nearby. She walked all the way around the block, trying every door. There was no bookstore on the block.

Shirley knew she had not imagined the incident, for she still had her copy of *Ardath*.

The Haunted Coal Mine

At Silverwood Colliery, in Yorkshire, England, miner Stephen Dimbleby had the most terrifying experience of his life.

Silverwood was a traditional coal mine. The men for each shift crowded into a big wire cage to be lowered down the shaft. When they reached the right level, they went off to work along the galleries that ran beneath the farming country above.

Late one Sunday night, around midnight, Stephen Dimbleby had been working in the mine with two colleagues. Then he went off on his own to collect some equipment from the end of a gallery that was temporarily abandoned. The shift was coming to an end. He was tired and looking forward to getting home for a hot meal.

As he walked back along the dimly lit gallery towards the main shaft, he suddenly noticed a figure ahead of him. He naturally assumed it was another miner, but he was puzzled. There were no side-tunnels along this gallery, so how could this other fellow have gotten there? It was probably one of his friends, he thought, fooling around.

The figure, walking slowly away from him, went around a bend and out of sight. Stephen walked faster. When he got to the bend, he called out "Hey!," but the man gave no sign of having heard him.

As he drew closer, Stephen noticed something decidedly odd. All miners wear helmets, but this man was wearing a funny old-fashioned helmet made from leather. Stephen could not remember seeing one like it.

Then he caught up with the man and touched him on the shoulder. The miner turned around. He was wearing an old dark vest over a T-shirt.

"When I shone my light on him," Stephen said, "there were no features on his face—just a smooth, pale blank below the helmet." This terrifying sight was more than Stephen Dimbleby could stand. "I just dropped my tackle and ran towards the shaft."

The next thing he remembers is waking up in the hospital. Co-workers told him later that they heard him screaming, "I've seen him! God help me, I've seen him!" He was frantic to get above ground.

The mine manager offered Stephen a surface job, and he took it, even though the pay was lower.

Some people think the phantom appears on the anniversary of a tragedy at the mine. Whatever it was, Stephen will never go down the pit again.

The Phantom Hotel

Some people claim it is possible to step back in time—to move through another dimension into a different era. They call it a time warp. Could that be what happened to two English couples in France in 1979?

The Simpsons and the Gisbys were already old friends the year they decided to drive together to Spain for their summer vacation. They crossed the English Channel and from Paris they drove southeast through wine country. They were tired by the time they reached the exit for Montelimar Nord, so they pulled off the highway and headed for the Motel Ibis nearby.

The Ibis was fully occupied, but the man at the desk suggested that they might take the old road towards Avignon. Only a short distance away was a small hotel where he felt sure there would be room.

They took his advice. They drove under the freeway, turned right at the fork in the road, and went past some construction and a striking billboard advertisement for matches. Then, a little way along on the left, in the gathering dusk, they spotted a building that looked like a small hotel. They knocked on the door, and were greeted with warmth and enthusiasm by the old couple inside.

Although they spoke no French, and the manager and his wife spoke no English, they discovered that there were rooms and they were welcome to stay. With relief they parked the car and carried their bags inside.

They went straight into the dining room, which had scrubbed wooden tables—primitive but clean. There was no menu, but Madame brought them a pleasant meal of rough greyish bread, soup, steak and vegetables.

After dinner they staggered wearily upstairs, to find bedrooms that were generations out of date. The beds were high platforms of wood. There were bolsters, but no pillows. The sheets were of stiff linen. The windows had wooden shutters, but no glass. The soap in the bathroom was fastened to the end of an iron bar, as though to keep it from being stolen.

They slept well and, in the morning before going downstairs, both husbands took pictures of their wives in the odd old bedrooms.

While they ate a breakfast of coffee and croissants, a woman came in to chat with their hosts. Cynthia Gisby was enchanted with the woman's antique clothes: a long skirt with a zigzag hem and high boots with many little buttons up the front. A policeman also stopped by to talk to the old couple. He was wearing a cape and a quaint tall helmet, the likes of which they had not seen before.

When they finished breakfast, the couples packed their things and asked for the bill. Madame gave them a piece of paper with just one amount on it—19F.

Nineteen francs was less than five dollars. "No, no!" they said, "The whole amount." And they made signs to show that they had eaten and drunk, spent the night and had breakfast. But Madame was adamant; the total was 19F. They gave her 20F and left.

*   *   *

They had a wonderful time in Spain. On the way back they decided to stay at the same place, since it had been fun and cheap. They took the exit for Montelimar Nord, turned under the freeway, right at the fork, past the construction and the billboard, and there on the left—nothing but empty fields.

They went on further, but arrived at another town. They turned back and looked again, but could see no sign of the hotel. Puzzled, they drove all the way back to the freeway, and started again. Still no trace. After two hours of hunting up and down the old road to Avignon, they gave up and stayed at the Motel Ibis, which this time was not full.

*   *   *

Every year they have returned to hunt for their cheap hotel, but never to this day have they found it.

Oh, yes—the photographs! Both cameras seem to have developed faults. Both Len Gisby and Colin Simpson had pictures of the north of France, before

Montelimar. On the end of the same roll of film each had pictures of the south of France, after Montelimar. But somehow neither camera had produced a picture in the old-fashioned hotel. There were no blank frames. The perforations were damaged—I looked at the negatives—but somehow there were no pictures on either film between north and south.

I went with them to search, one year, along with a local expert from the French Tourist Board, who brought a list of all the hotels in the area. To begin with, he believed they had simply lost their way. But we looked all day and still found no trace of their cheap hotel.

So was it a phantom hotel? Could it really be that in 1979 they drove through a gap in the fabric of time?

The Missing Hole

The Rev. Alfred Byles had just become vicar in Yealmpton (pronounced "Yampton"), a small town near Plymouth, England. One morning he was making his way up the steep hill towards the side door of his church.

As he walked up through the graveyard, he found a hole in the middle of the gravel path. It was about three feet across, and quite deep—a pretty large pothole!

His first thought was that someone might fall in and be hurt. He hurried into the church, where his wife was arranging flowers, and called her out to see it.

By the time they got back to the hole, it was much bigger—about six feet wide. It extended right across the gravel path between the gravestones, and into the grass on either side. They threw in a couple of pebbles, which disappeared without trace.

Looking into the hole, the Byleses thought they could make out something solid, like big rocks, as though part of a wall or other structure were underneath. The vicar wanted to climb down and investigate, but his wife pointed out that they couldn't see the bottom clearly, that it certainly was deep, and that it might well sink down even further.

Mrs. Byles went back to work on the flowers in the church. The vicar went up into the village. On the main street, about 200 yards from the church, he met Mr. Knight, a local builder and undertaker, just the man to set some planks across the hole to prevent anyone from falling in.

Together they walked back to the churchyard—but the hole was gone! The gravel path was as smooth and level as it had ever been. The grass on each side was undisturbed.

Mr. Byles, shocked, called his wife, "Come quickly. The hole! It's gone!"

"What do you mean, the hole has gone?" Mrs. Byles couldn't believe her eyes. "Where has it gone?"

Only Mr. Knight said nothing—and never mentioned the hole again. Was it perhaps because something similar had happened there before?

2. UNBELIEVABLE!

Some stories you have to take with a pinch of salt—they are too weird to be true. What about these next four?

Fish from the Sky

Marksville, Louisiana, is a small southern town where everyone knows everyone else. Families live for generations in the same houses—wooden houses, white-painted, with wide verandas against the southern heat. Usually nothing much unexpected happens in small towns, but in downtown Marksville, on October 23, 1947, at about 8:30 in the morning, fish came falling from the sky.

Mrs. Eddie Gremillion was sick in bed when her maid came running in, shouting that it was raining fishes. Mrs. Elmire Roy's maid said it must be the end of the world. Eleanor Gremillion reckons the fish were six or seven inches long, Daphne Richard thinks five or six.

Sheriff Potch Didier was driving a patrol car along the street when he saw fish bouncing in the yards on his right, and then on his left, and on the road in front of him. He could not make out where they were coming from; so he got out of the car, and found they were raining down. "I was amazed," he told me. "I was very amazed."

Bob Neitzel saw them in the street, right outside the offices of the local paper, *The Weekly News*, which was ironic because the *News* had just gone to press. They had had a phone call 20 minutes earlier that fish were falling from the sky. The editor dismissed it as a hoax, and went ahead printing the paper.

Two brothers, Anthony ("Sookie") and Chris Roy were walking to school. One fish hit Sookie on the head. Chris is now a lawyer, and Sookie is president of the CenLa bank.

How in the world can fish fall from the sky? There were plenty of theories. One witness claimed to have seen a flock of pelicans flying overhead shortly before the fish fell. Maybe they were all carrying fish in their beaks and were frightened into dropping them.

Now, pelicans are common in the area, and they certainly carry fish, but why should a flock all drop their fish at once? And hundreds of fish were seen to fall. It's hard to believe that dozens of bulging-beaked pelicans would collect for a precision bombing run.

The tornado theory seems more likely. Twisters are well known in warm, damp Louisiana. Maybe a twister travelled over one of the bayous in the area where it could have picked up water and fish at the same time. When the energy wound down a few miles later, perhaps it dumped the fish on the town.

Or maybe you have a better explanation?

The Italian Bride

The Italian Bride was buried 70 years ago, yet they say that her ghost still walks along the paths through Mt. Carmel Cemetery in Chicago, trailing the scent of roses from her wedding bouquet.

Julia Buccola Petta was a beautiful girl. She fell in love and was married to the man of her dreams. Then tragedy struck in 1921, when she died in childbirth at the age of 29.

Following Chicago Italian tradition, she was buried in her wedding dress. A life-size stone monument depicts her as a bride, and a photograph mounted on her tombstone shows her in a long, full-skirted white gown, carrying a bouquet of roses.

A year after her death, her mother, Philomena, had a disturbing dream, in which Julia begged her to have her body exhumed. Philomena could not understand this, and did not take it seriously until she had another dream, and then another. A whole series of these unusual dreams at last suggested that her daughter was unhappy in her grave; so she pleaded with authorities to have the body dug up.

This was not a request to be granted lightly, and by the time permission was granted, five years had passed.

Eventually, in 1927, the grave was opened and the casket removed. When they lifted the lid, they found Julia's body in perfect condition—as pink and fresh as it was on the day she died. The onlookers were astonished, and the body was photographed in its casket. This photograph is also displayed on Julia's tombstone.

Apparently, when the body was laid to rest for a second time, the ghost found peace, for her mother reported no further terrible dreams.

And yet even today some visitors to the cemetery have reported seeing a lonely figure walking along the pavement in a long white dress, and many passers-by have reported smelling the scent of fresh roses in the vicinity of her tomb, even though none grow anywhere nearby.

"The different scents are quite distinctive, and these were definitely baby roses—tea roses," said floral designer Ruth Bukowski, after she visited the grave in November 1982. No roses bloom there in November.

Should we conclude that the Italian Bride is at last at rest? Why then doesn't she leave the graveyard and take the roses with her?

Resurrection Mary

Ghosts rarely pair off at dances and let their escorts take them home. Resurrection Mary is an exception. She appears to "live" in the huge Polish cemetery in the western suburbs of Chicago called Resurrection Cemetery, and she has caused quite a number of hearts to flutter during the last 60 years.

According to Jerry Palus, she is a beautiful blonde Polish-American girl. The night he met her she was wearing a long white ball gown, and her hair was in ringlets. "It hung down around her head like Polish sausages," Jerry said. This was in 1939 at a dance at Liberty Grove. They danced together most of the evening. Her hand, Jerry said, was as cold as ice. So was the small of her back.

When the dancing stopped, he asked if he could

drive her home, and was delighted when she agreed. She directed him to Archer Road. There she asked him to pull off by the side of the road, said she had to get out, and told him not to follow her. Then she skipped out of the car, darted across the street, and disappeared through the closed gates of Resurrection Cemetery.

Only then did Jerry begin to wonder about her ice-cold body. He had once been a funeral director and embalmer, and he suddenly realized that such cold flesh could not have belonged to a living girl.

*　　*　　*

Resurrection Mary is unusual in several ways. Ghosts are rarely seen by more than one person—almost never by two people at the same time. But late one night, Shawn and Geri Lape were driving down Archer, past the cemetery, when they saw a girl in a white dress running across the street. She seemed to be trying to slip through the heavy traffic, but she misjudged the speed of their car. Shawn jammed on the brakes as hard as he could—rubber screeched on the road—but the couple watched helplessly as the girl disappeared beneath their hood.

There was no crash or bump—just the awful silence that always follows an accident. All the traffic slowed to a halt. Shawn and Geri rushed out and looked, but there was no sign of any person under the car, nor beside the road—no sign of anything at all. The girl had vanished, leaving not a mark on the street, nor on the car.

Perhaps Mary lived before the age of the automobile, when crossing the road was less dangerous? Or perhaps she just likes to scare people; she certainly succeeded in scaring the Lapes.

Yet another strange feature of the Resurrection Mary story is that the beautiful blonde phantom evidently has phenomenal strength. Ask Police Sergeant Pat Homer. He went to the cemetery in his squad car in August 1976, in answer to a distress call about a blonde girl in a white dress who was reported to be locked inside. When he got there he could see no sign of the girl, but he noticed something that sent chills down his spine.

Hand prints had been pressed into the bronze bars of the cemetery gates—small hand prints, such as might have belonged to a young woman. But no human hands could possibly have made an impression on those bars. Pat Homer was left with the terrifying conclusion that here at last were physical traces of Resurrection Mary.

The Ju-Ju

During World War Two, a West African soldier in Burma asked for an interview with his colonel and requested immediate leave. He had to get home the following day, he said. A Ju-Ju was coming, and he had to be in his house, in his village in West Africa, to meet it.

A Ju-Ju, the soldier explained, was an evil spirit, an all-powerful menace, probably conjured up by an enemy with the help of a witch-doctor. It might come in the guise of a person, or of a goat, but perhaps it would be just a wicked wraith in a whirl of dust. The vital thing was that he had to be home to defend himself.

The colonel regretted that this was impossible. Even if he gave the man immediate leave, there was no way he could get from Burma to West Africa in 24 hours.

The soldier's eyes rolled in alarm. "If I no go to Ju-Ju, Ju-Ju go come to me; I go die."

Dismissed by the colonel, he went to the mobile hospital and announced that he was going to die. Surprised, the orderly wrote down his name, rank, and number.

In the admissions tent he was examined by Captain Alf Lewis. The young, fit-looking fellow lay on a stretcher-bed, flat on his back, calm and still, looking at the tent roof. He wouldn't answer any questions and he did not speak, but his pulse was regular, his respiration was fine, his temperature was normal. There seemed to be nothing wrong with him—or, at least, nothing medically wrong.

The doctor wasn't worried. The human body has automatic systems to keep it going. When you lose consciousness, your heart beats and you breathe without conscious effort. Even if you hold your breath until you faint, you won't die. Your system is designed to operate on automatic. You cannot just decide to stop functioning; your body won't allow it.

The next day, around 12:30 in the afternoon, Alf Lewis had a phone call from the major in the field ambulance. Just after noon, the soldier from West Africa had stopped breathing, closed his eyes, and died.

His Ju-Ju had come.

3. HAUNTED HOUSES

Traditional ghosts are often seen in haunted houses. According to one theory, a dead person's image, or spirit, may be recorded in the fabric of the building and then replayed when the time is right, as though the stones or bricks were acting like videotape.

If this theory were correct, you might expect to see a headless lady in the blue bedroom of the castle, because that is her home. You would not expect to see her anywhere else; nor would you expect to see a faceless monk in the same chamber.

Some houses may be haunted because their walls are easily imprinted—naturally sensitive to evil. Or perhaps any house could be affected by a terrible deed, despair or death. What do you think?

The House by Weir Lake

The Bradford house on the waterfront at Oklawaha, Florida, looks like a peaceful summer home. Water laps at the wooden jetty. The orange trees in the yard sway gently against the blue sky. There is nothing to alert the casual visitor to the sinister character of the property.

Elizabeth Ternent and her daughter Betty Ann Good, who bought the house, began hearing noises soon after they arrived. First they heard footsteps on the stairs. Then, when they were sitting downstairs, they heard footsteps on the floorboards above, but when they went to look there would be nobody there.

"Then there were times we would hear someone downstairs playing cards," said Mrs. Ternent. "It was like a lot of people, not just three or four. And there was a lot of talking—loud talking—so loud that you could almost hear what they were saying, but you couldn't quite catch the words. You'd hear the arguments, and you'd hear the chips going down on the table—but you could never find anyone there when you ran down."

Mrs. Good recalls that one weekend three teenage boys, sharing the green bedroom, were woken in the middle of the night by a strange scratching noise. In the morning they swore on a Bible that it was a woman, sitting on the end of the bed, combing her long hair. . . .

The owners found a clue in the walls and the doors, for the plaster and woodwork show signs of bullet holes. When they inquired into the history of the house, its violent past was revealed.

Late in 1934 the house was rented by a "Mrs. Blackburn," whose real name was Kate Barker, known to the FBI as "America's Deadliest Woman." Their "wanted" posters showed her as a handsome woman with long dark hair. She and her three gangster sons had chosen this house as their hideout, but the FBI tracked them down.

On January 16, 1935 the Bradford house was the scene of the longest shoot-out in FBI history. All morning the federal officers were held at bay by a hail of tommy-gun bullets. So fierce was the barrage they assumed they had trapped the whole gang, though in fact the two elder boys were away, leaving only "Ma" Barker and her youngest son, Freddy.

Eventually they were gunned down—Ma Barker in the green bedroom, Freddy on the stairs. Their bodies were carted off to the mortuary, but it appears that their ghosts have stayed behind, in the very place where they died.

The Roman Soldiers

Right behind York Minster, one of the finest cathedrals in northern Europe, stands the Treasurer's House, one of the world's most haunted places.

There are many ghosts. Visitors have admitted trying to follow a liveried footman through a blank wall where there used to be a door. A figure in armor has been reported on the battlements outside.

And, in a window just above the street, a little girl is often seen silently weeping. Three hundred years ago, the family who lived there fell victim to the plague. One by one they died, until only the little girl was left. She did not catch the dread disease, but she was too frightened to go out for food, and no one dared go in. Then, to isolate the plague victims, they walled up the doorway, leaving her inside to starve.

But of all the ghostly visitors, the strangest were seen in a small cellar.

In 1953 Harry Martindale was in this cellar fixing

some heating pipes. He was on a ladder, a few feet off the ground, when he heard the shrill blast of a trumpet. As he looked down, a figure came straight through the wall.

Harry can't remember how he got from the ladder into the corner of the room, but there he crouched without daring to breathe as a column of Roman soldiers marched across the cellar. They came in through one wall, crossed the room, and went out the opposite wall.

The first man was leading a horse, on which another soldier was riding. After the horse came the foot soldiers. Many had beards sticking out beside the chinstraps of their helmets. Each carried a short sword. They wore broad strips of leather fastened together to make jerkins and knee-length green skirts.

Harry was terrified they would attack him, for they marched past only a few feet away. Yet not one of them even looked in his direction; it was as though they were travelling in a different dimension of time.

Most curious of all, he could not see anything below their knees. Only in the center of the room, where a hole had been dug in the floor, could he briefly glimpse details of their stockings, sandals, and leather straps. This puzzled him greatly. How could these so-called soldiers march with their feet underground?

The reason became clear when Harry found out that the hole had been dug by archaeologists. The Treasurer's House stood right on the main road that led into the army camp at the Roman city of Eboracum. When they excavated the cellar floor they found that under eighteen inches of rubble was the perfectly preserved surface of the old Roman road.

The Horror of Hawk Mountain

Ornithologist Seth Benz was a rational young scientist, not given to wild imagination. He certainly did not believe in ghosts, until he came to the house on Hawk Mountain.

He moved to Hawk Mountain, Pennsylvania, as warden of the bird sanctuary, a beautiful spot where every year thousands of birds stop to feed and to rest. He lived alone, quietly, and looked forward to the solitude and the natural wilderness of the area.

One evening after a light supper he was washing the dishes in the kitchen. He turned to make sure that none were left, when he heard a switch go CLICK, and the lights went out. Then, after a few seconds' silence—CLICK, and they came on again.

He was alone in the house. No one else could have come in, and in any case the light switch was within his sight in the kitchen. Maybe a short in the electrical system, he thought—but how on earth could that make the clicks of the light switch?

A few days later he was in the kitchen again. The evening was still. He heard footsteps on the wooden stairs. They started at the bottom, and moved slowly up to the top. Again he knew there was no one else in the house, and from where he stood the stairs were in sight. He could see there was no one on them, even while he could hear the footsteps. The next morning Benz told his colleagues about the odd happenings.

"I'm not surprised," said old Tom, who had been around longer than anyone could remember. "Didn't they tell you about the house? It used to be an inn, where travellers stopped. Trouble was, some of them stopped a good deal longer than they wanted."

Everyone turned to old Tom. "What do you mean?"

"Seems like the landlord was a handy man with an axe. Probably had quite a few murders to his credit. Fellow named Shumacher—no, Schambacher—Matthias Schambacher. The law got him in the end."

That evening, May 15th, Benz had a couple of friends in to visit. He had barely poured out a glass of wine when they all heard steps running up the stairs; it sounded like one man chasing another. There were sounds of a desperate struggle above, and a terrible hoarse cry came echoing down the stairs.

Then nothing.

When they went to look they could find no trace of anyone upstairs. But next day Seth looked up the local records, and found that Matthias Schambacher had committed his last murder one hundred years earlier—on May 15th.

A Ghost of the Living

Ted Simon is a journalist who writes for *The Times* in London. He went around the world on a motorcycle and wrote a book about his experiences. He is a trained observer, used to recording facts.

In 1983 Simon sent to *The Times* an account of how he had seen a ghost of a living person; curiously, ghosts of the living seem to be even more common than ghosts of the dead.

One evening he went with his wife and son to visit an old friend of his mother's, a kindly middle-aged widow. He had not announced that they were coming. They just drove there and walked up to the front door. She wouldn't mind, he was sure. She was always delighted to see them, and would probably offer them a cup of tea, or perhaps a glass of sherry.

The house was set back a little from the road, and as they walked up the short drive in the dusk, he noticed that the lights were on in the hall and in the kitchen. He rang the bell, and waited.

She did not come to the door, so he rang again. He could hear the bell ring in the kitchen. But still there was no reply.

He stood on tiptoe, so that he could see in through the window. As he watched, he saw the widow quite clearly coming through from the kitchen across the living room towards the front door. "Here she comes," he said, and went back to the front door, but still it did not open.

He knocked, and rang again, but to no avail. He saw her briefly once more, walking back to the kitchen, her bouffant hairstyle clearly backlit by the kitchen light. Again she paid no heed to his knocking.

Ted and his wife went to the village, found a phone, and dialed her number; but there was no reply. Ted was intensely puzzled, but he did not pursue the matter until the next day.

In the morning he phoned again. His mother's friend answered at once, and recognized his voice with affection. "There you are!" Ted said, much relieved. "What was wrong yesterday? Why wouldn't you answer the door?"

She was surprised. "What on earth are you talking about?" Ted explained how he had tried to visit her, but had been unable to attract her attention.

Now she was amazed. "I was away visiting my daughter. There's no way you could have seen me at home."

"But I did! I saw you through the window!" he said.

"Not me; I left the lights on for the burglars, but I was away all day."

What *did* Ted see through the window that afternoon? What do you think?

4. TRAVELLING GHOSTS

The idea that violent deaths or other terrible happenings may leave psychic impressions behind them—like magnetic impressions in videotape—is called the stone-tape theory. Certainly some specters seem to stay in a single place; they are reported regularly in a particular house or cemetery. But others seem to be restless.

How can you explain ghosts that actively travel on the highways—by car and by bus?

Many of them seem especially to enjoy hitchhiking!

Backseat Driver

Mabel Chinery lived with her husband, Jim, in a retirement home in Ipswich, on the east coast of England. While her mother was alive, they liked to take her out for a drive in their car on Sunday afternoons.

In 1959 the old lady died. She was buried in the local churchyard.

Two weeks later Mabel and Jim visited the graveyard, and after Mabel had tidied the flowers, Jim took a picture of the grave. There was one picture left on the roll; so Mabel took a shot of Jim sitting behind the wheel, getting ready to drive home.

When the film came back after processing, the pictures were as they expected, all except for the last one. It showed Jim in the driver's seat, but it also showed another figure. Over Jim's shoulder, dimly in the back seat, was the face of Mabel's mother.

All Jim could think of were her last words to him: "Don't worry, Jim. I shall always be with you!"

Out of Gas

Once upon a time there was an actor, world famous for his role as a TV law enforcement officer. Let's call him Terry.

He was driving home late one night, after a party near New York City, when he ran out of gas. It can happen to anyone—even the rich and famous.

He pulled over to the side of the road. The place was lonely, so he reckoned he would have to walk several miles to a gas station, even if he could find one open. To make matters worse, he had no money on him. At least he had a can for carrying the gas, but that wouldn't save him the walk.

He was just setting off into the darkness when a pair of headlights came around the corner and a great black limo pulled up beside him. The window purred down, and the driver leaned across.

"You got a problem?"

"Yeah!" he said, "I ran out of gas."

"OK—hop in. Let's go. Hey, haven't I seen you on TV?"

Terry sighed, but being recognized was a small price to pay for a ride to the gas station. The stranger turned out to be kind: he not only paid for the gas, but also drove Terry all the way back to his car.

Terry thanked him, insisting that he would repay the money for the gas. The stranger produced a card, on which he wrote his address. Then he thanked Terry for his company and conversation, and drove off.

Terry got his car started, and eventually got home to bed.

The next day he had a couple of hours to spare after rehearsal, and he decided to drive out to the good Samaritan's home, and repay the money in person. He found the house and knocked on the door.

The woman who answered seemed surprised to see him, and amazed when he told her what had happened the night before. She asked to see the card. When she saw it, she trembled, and burst into tears. Recovering, she agreed that it was her husband's handwriting.

"But he could not have given you this card," she said. "He was run down in the street—by a big black car that didn't stop. He died exactly a year ago last night."

The Archangel Gabriel

The phantom hitchhiker appears in many shapes and forms, in many cultures and in many countries. Either people hallucinate a great deal when they drive, or there really is an army of ghosts standing beside the highways of the world with their phantom thumbs extended.

Perhaps the strangest tale I have been told came from a woman who lived in Bavaria, in the southeast corner of Germany.

She was driving towards Munich one evening in 1983 when she saw a man standing beside the road, trying to get a lift. It was cold and dark and raining, so she stopped to let him in.

She wanted to change her mind when she saw that he had a long straggly beard and was dressed in a robe and sandals, but she reluctantly let him into the car.

"Fasten your seat belt," she said, but he couldn't do it, because she had put her seat belt buckle into his socket. So she had to unbuckle her own belt in order to let the hitch-hiker fasten his.

They set off, talking about the weather. Then she passed a truck on a narrow stretch of road, and focused exclusively on her driving for a few seconds. Nevertheless, she was dimly aware of her passenger saying, "I think you should know that I am the Archangel Gabriel. I have come to tell you that the world is going to end on October 31st next year."

She heard the words, but couldn't take in their meaning until she had passed the truck. Then she realized her passenger was very unusual indeed, and she turned to speak to him.

The seat was empty.

But the seat belt was still fastened.

The Little Old Lady in the Leopardskin Dress

Trevor Pease worked for many years as a bus conductor for Plymouth Corporation, in the southwest corner of England. His job was to help passengers on and off the buses and sell them tickets.

One summer day he was on his normal route, number 19, heading into town from the east, and they stopped to pick up a family in the suburbs. There were two couples and an elderly lady. They took some time asking whether the bus would take them into the center of town, and how long the trip would take; so Trevor had a good look at them.

As far as he could tell, the two middle-aged women were sisters, and the men were their husbands. The old woman must have been the mother of the two sisters, since the family likeness was strong.

The old woman was dressed in a startling outfit of fake leopardskin, with a turquoise butterfly brooch, and matching shoes and handbag—smart, but rather loud for Plymouth.

The rest of the family seemed to ignore her. They all climbed up to the top deck of the bus, leaving her to go up last. She gave him a shrug and a wink as she went up the spiral stair.

When he went up to collect the fares, one of the men asked for four tickets to the city center. Trevor could see no sign of the old lady. He walked all the way to the front, half expecting her to jump out from behind a seat, but he couldn't see her anywhere.

He sold the passengers four tickets, but said, "You know there were five of you when you got on, don't you?"

When they reached their destination and were getting off, one of the women asked Trevor what he had meant—who was the fifth person? So he described the old lady, and her outfit, and said he had assumed she was their mother.

The woman looked uncomfortable. "You're right," she said. "She was our mother, and the outfit is exactly what she wore the last time we all went out together. That was ten years ago, the day before she died."

5. POLTERGEISTS

Most ghosts tend to be seen but not heard. They flit silently from room to room, dematerialize, and slide through solid walls. But when there is a poltergeist in the house you *know* it.

Poltergeist is a German word; it means noisy spirit. Poltergeists are not seen, but they leave wreckage in their path. Usually, things get upset and broken. Furniture may be turned over—the contents of bottles and jars may be spilled. Crockery may fly around the room. Electrical equipment may go crazy.

Often the disturbances seem to be centered around a "focus person"—usually a teenager. But this does not seem to make the problem much easier to solve.

Poltergeists can cause terrible disruption—particularly to the lives of those nearby. Usually, the best remedy seems to be grin and bear it.

The Swinging Lamps

Poltergeists have been reported for hundreds of years, but perhaps the most famous case of all comes, appropriately, from Germany.

Sigmund Adam was a lawyer in the market town of Rosenheim, not far from the Austrian border. He employed five people in his offices on the third floor of a large, old building.

In late 1967 the peace and quiet of the office was shattered by a series of weird events that even to this day have not been fully explained.

There were four telephones in the office, and the staff noticed that their conversations were frequently interrupted by loud buzzes and clicks. Sometimes a phone rang, but there was no one there. Then all the phones rang simultaneously, but still there was no one at the other end.

The phone bill was enormously high. Herr Adam summoned the phone company, had all the wiring checked, all the phones replaced, and a separate meter installed on every phone to find out who was making the calls. To no avail—the mysterious phenomena continued.

Stranger still, they heard the meters clicking up calls even when the phones were not being used!

The next phone bill was itemized. It showed the time and duration of every call. Apparently, hundreds of calls had been made to 0119, which was the number of the time check. At one point 0119 was being called more than five times a minute. Herr Adam and his colleagues tried dialling 0119, and found it was impossible to do it more than three times in a minute—even if they didn't wait for the connection to be made in between calls.

Meanwhile, other strange things happened. The photocopying machine leaked fluid on the floor. A drawer slid out of an unoccupied desk, and the petty cash box jumped out and scattered money across the office.

Most of the light fixtures were fluorescent tubes. Some of them were seen to twist in their sockets and then explode. The rest had to be covered with wire netting for safety.

Two large heavy pictures rotated on the wall. They remained flat, but spun through 360 degrees while the staff watched, goggle-eyed.

But the most curious thing of all was that nothing unusual happened when 19-year-old office clerk Annemarie Schwabel was away from the office.

Then they noticed that when Annemarie walked to the bathroom, the lamps would swing in the hall above her head. These lamps were too high for her to reach, but apparently began to swing all by themselves as she passed by.

The phone company could not help; electrical engineers could do nothing; the police had no clear crime to investigate. In desperation Herr Adam called in Hans Bender, Professor of Parapsychology. Bender confirmed that this was a poltergeist at work, and that Annemarie seemed unknowingly to be the focus-person.

Bender suggested that Annemarie find another job. When she left the lawyer's office, the extraordinary events stopped. She is now happily married with two children, and has been untroubled by poltergeists for more than 20 years.

Rain of Rocks

Thornton Road is a quiet suburb of Birmingham, England, but in 1981, five houses there came under siege from rocks thrown by an unknown hand.

It started in May when one of the residents, sitting in his back yard, was startled to hear a THUMP behind him. Turning round, he saw a rock on the path. He could see no one in the other yards nearby, but he suspected one of his neighbors of fooling around—dangerously.

A few days later another person was almost hit by a stone, and then windows were broken in several of the houses. Eventually, a stone came straight through a window and grazed the head of the man inside. Mr. Malcolm started wearing his army helmet just to hang the wash on the line.

The police were called in July 1981, but the attacks

continued. In October Chief Inspector Len Turley was put on the case. At first he thought that a couple of investigating officers would solve the mystery in a week or two. He was wrong.

The stones that caused the damage were generally smooth round pebbles, about three inches across. A dozen or two are still in police custody. They look as though they come from the beach, but, in fact, smooth pebbles like these were lying around in all the gardens in the area. The strange thing is that all the stones that were thrown at houses seemed to have been washed or scrubbed—they had no dirt on them, no marks, and no fingerprints!

Naturally enough, the police thought at first that a person or people must be throwing the stones, and tried everything they could think of to track down the culprits. They used automatic cameras to try to catch a stone-thrower in the act. They set up infrared equipment to watch in total darkness from the windows. They got nothing but blank film.

They drew maps and plans, calculated trajectories, and worked out from what distances and angles the stones might possibly have come. They considered every possibility of catapults and launchers.

Police officers spent many long cold hours standing in the gardens and on the roofs, watching the houses. Occasionally they heard what sounded like a stone striking a building, but all they saw were rabbits and a fox. The weather was so cold that one officer, Danny McMahon, took a flask of hot soup with him. By the time he opened the flask the soup was frozen solid.

During 1982 the area police arrested 1998 criminals. They solved five murder cases, two of them very complicated. They were a highly professional team. Yet after 3,500 man-hours of investigations in Thornton Road, they were no nearer to solving the mystery of the raining rocks.

No one was badly injured by the stones, though serious damage was done to the properties. The owners spent thousands of dollars replacing smashed glass and tiles.

Finally, the backs of numbers 30–38 had to be boarded up and guarded with wire netting—to protect the glass in the windows.

The effect on the nerves of the residents was even worse. Mrs. Malcolm recalls going out just as it was getting dark to get a pair of pants from the clothesline. "It's uncanny," she said. "It's as though someone's watching you all the time . . ." As she stepped back inside, a stone thumped into the wall by the back door, barely missing her head.

The Sliding Stones of Racetrack Playa

Death Valley, the most famous desert in the United States, lies on the eastern edge of California, just inside the border from Nevada. It's a lonely place. There are clusters of houses at Stovepipe Wells and Furnace Creek, but the Upper Mojave Desert phone book contains only seven small pages.

Drive north 50 miles from Furnace Creek, and you come to a fork in the road near the Grapevine ranger station. The right fork goes to Scotty's Castle; the left leads past Ubehebe Crater to Teakettle Junction and eventually, after three hours of gravel road, to Racetrack Playa.

The Spanish word *playa* means dry lake bed. Racetrack is like a barren table. About a mile wide and one and a half miles long, it is surrounded by bare brown mountains. The surface is dead flat—perhaps an inch higher at the north end than at the south. The mud is hard, cracked into crazy pentagons and hexagons by the heat of the sun.

There is no green in sight. The earth is brown, the sky is blue. It's a two-tone universe. To go behind a bush you would have to walk five miles. Even to go behind a mound of earth you would have to walk two miles.

Lying about on the mud surface are rocks that have rolled off the mountains. They vary in size from pebbles an inch across to 500-pound boulders.

And here lies the mystery, for many of these rocks seem to move about in the night.

Early in the morning, when the sun climbs over the rim of the mountains, the shadows are long on the mud surface. Behind many of the stones can be seen long trails, showing where they have slid into their present positions.

Some stones have moved only a foot or two; some have moved two or three hundred feet. They slide in nearly-straight lines, or in slight curves; though, in rare cases, they seem to change direction through sharp angles.

Scientists have studied this phenomenon in detail. They have found that on average a stone moves about once a year, and that the tracks of the stones are often nearly parallel. This suggested the idea that perhaps the rocks get frozen in sheets of ice that then slide across the playa.

The ice theory has now been disproved. On two separate occasions a stone that was inside a corral of steel stakes moved out. This would be impossible if it had been frozen in a sheet of ice.

Rain seems a more likely cause. On the rare occasions when it falls, it stirs up a thin watery mixture of very slippery clay—so slippery that you can't stand on it. Perhaps when the playa is wet, the stones may begin to slide under the influence of strong winds, and then ride on cushions of slippery clay, leaving trails behind them.

Yet no one has ever reported seeing a stone move.

6. DIRECT FROM MIND TO MIND

Some people seem to be able to communicate without speaking to one another, or even seeing one another. The transfer of information without using the normal senses—apparently direct from mind to mind—is called telepathy or extra-sensory perception (ESP for short).

Sometimes you may think about making contact with a friend; the telephone rings, and your friend has called you. This can be quite a surprise when it happens. Unfortunately, you can't prove what you were thinking about before the phone rang—so you cannot prove most cases of ESP.

Only occasionally are such events well documented, and that is what these stories are about: extraordinary evidence that telepathy is real.

The Hospital Gown

Shirley Gray was woken up in the middle of one night in 1977 by a voice calling her name. As she sat up in bed, she saw the head and shoulders of her friend Pat Craven, as though she were standing at the foot of the bed. Pat was clearly in great distress; she looked haggard and in pain.

Shirley had no idea what was worrying her friend, but was amazed by what Pat Craven was wearing.

"Pat is always smart—a really snappy dresser—and she had on something she wouldn't normally be seen dead in." Shirley described it, "like a T-shirt, square across the shoulders and with absolutely no shape to it." The round neck was either ragged or frilly.

Shirley couldn't make out what Pat was trying to tell her, but the apparition faded, and eventually she went back to sleep.

In the morning, when she called her friend, she found out Pat was away on a tour in Kenya. When she returned with her husband, her luggage, and a spectacular suntan, Shirley was on the phone within the hour:

"Whatever happened to you?"

Pat Craven was astonished. She had suffered a slightly embarrassing accident while in Kenya, and hadn't told anyone about it. She had no idea how news could have reached her friend Shirley, 4,000 miles away in England.

The outcome of the accident was that her Achilles tendon had been injured, and she went to a hospital in Mombasa for a minor operation. For this operation she had worn a simple hospital gown. It had a top like a simple T-shirt, with square shoulders, shapeless sides, and a ragged round neck.

Thoughts Through Space

Harold Sherman was a sportswriter for the *New York Times*. Sir Hubert Wilkins was an Australian aviator. One day in 1937, in the City Club in New York, they agreed to try one of the strangest experiments in telepathy that has ever been recorded.

The Russian government was attempting to set up a new commercial air route between Moscow and the United States, and during a trial flight one of their planes had disappeared somewhere in the Arctic wastes of Alaska. They had hired Wilkins to search for the plane.

Communication between Wilkins and his base in New York was clearly going to be difficult. They had radio, but radio is notoriously unreliable in those high latitudes where swirling magnetic fields light the sky with the aurora borealis and throw the compass out of joint.

Wilkins agreed that every Monday, Tuesday, and Thursday evening, at 11:30 p.m. New York time, he would sit down quietly on his own and review the events of the day—think through in his mind the dramatic things he had seen. At precisely the same time Sherman would sit in a darkened room in his apartment in New York City, with his reporter's notebook at hand to jot down the impressions that came into his head.

Wilkins never found the Russian plane. But the telepathy experiment produced some astonishing successes. Here are four of them:

On November 11 Sherman wrote that he saw Wilkins in a dinner suit, going reluctantly to a fancy dinner with many military men and women in evening dress. Sherman didn't believe his own vision, since Wilkins was on a rescue mission, and would hardly have taken a tuxedo with him.

He found out that, forced down by bad weather at Regina, Wilkins had tea with the Governor of Saskatchewan, and stayed on for the Armistice Ball that evening. The Governor loaned him a tuxedo. The other guests included many army and police officers in uniform.

Sherman wrote "Someone seems to put or pin something on your coat lapel. . . ."

It turned out that, at a formal breakfast in Winnipeg, Wilkins was given a city badge, which was pinned on his coat.

On December 7 Sherman had the impression of a fire. He wrote "Get definite fire impression as though house burning; you can see it from your location."

He found out later that Wilkins was in the radio office at Point Barrow when the fire alarm rang, at precisely 11:30 p.m. New York Time. He went to a window, and looked out at the village. An Eskimo house was on fire. Flames were roaring out of the chimney, and they spread quickly to the roof where it was free of snow.

Point Barrow is on the Arctic Ocean, on the north coast of Alaska, nearly 3,500 miles from New York City.

On January 27 Wilkins came upon a dead dog on the ice, shot through the head. This disturbed him greatly. The people in that area treasure their dogs, and to find one that had been killed was like coming across a murder victim. This strong feeling seemed to go straight through the ether to Sherman's receptive mind, for he wrote, "A dog seems to have been injured and had to be shot. Quite a strong feeling here."

The *New York Times* had their own radio operator to pick up Wilkins's dispatches. His name was Reg Iversen, and he told me that Sherman got more and better information by telepathy than he was able to get by radio.

The Blue Orchid of Table Mountain

Georgina Feakes had no brothers or sisters, but she was often invited over by her aunt Beatrice Howison to play with her cousin Owen. They became close friends.

In the late 1930s, the Howison family moved to South Africa, and when World War Two began, Owen volunteered to serve in a tank regiment. He went to Italy, and in 1944 was posted missing in action.

Soon after, Georgina was sitting in her home in southeastern England when she felt a sudden pain in her head and heard a buzzing noise. Then, she says, there appeared in the room in front of her a ball of golden mist, in which she could make out the shape of Owen's head and shoulders.

She was frozen—unable to move—as he said, "Tell Mum my tank's been hit, but I feel perfectly all right. And please give my love to poor Helen."

Georgina forced herself to speak. "Give me proof—I must have proof," she said, because she knew her aunt would be skeptical about news from such a source.

Owen said "Watch!" Then he opened his shirt, and took out a beautiful blue flower. He put it back inside his shirt again, and then he took it out once more. It was no ordinary flower—it had rich, vivid petals, and a penetrating sweet scent that filled the room. Then Owen and the ball of golden mist faded gradually from her sight.

Georgina wrote with excitement to her aunt in South Africa, and Beatrice wrote back: "Thank you for this wonderful proof, with evidence of which you could not possibly have been aware." And she explained.

On his last leave home, Owen had climbed Table Mountain, which his mother could not do because of her arthritis. On the mountain he found and picked a rare blue orchid. These orchids grow only on Table Mountain and are protected by law; the penalty for picking one was a large fine or even imprisonment.

So when he took the flower for his mother, Owen hid it in his shirt. He brought it out to show to her, but he was startled by a door banging in the house. He hid it away once more, and only when he was sure the coast was clear did he take it out again.

Beatrice had not written to England about the flower, since all letters were opened by the censor, and she didn't dare risk the penalty for picking the flower. So there was no way Georgina could possibly have known about the blue orchid by any normal means.

They found out later that Owen had in fact been killed when his tank suffered a direct hit. Why, then, did he say he felt "all right"? Could it have been because his spirit was at peace?

One mystery remained. Owen had said, "Give my love to poor Helen," but who was Helen? Owen's mother knew of no one by that name. She went through all Owen's things, and found no letters from Helen, or even from an "H".

But there was a Helen, Helen Hart. Owen had met her just before he went to war. They had become very close very quickly, and when he left, he wrote her letters and poems. Their love was so fresh and new that they had not even told their parents.

It was only when the story of the young hero and the blue orchid leaked out to the press and appeared in newspapers in South Africa, that Helen Hart got in touch with Beatrice, and showed her some of Owen's letters. And so it was that because of the blue orchid, Beatrice was able to carry out Owen's last request and give his love to poor Helen.

7. STRANGE POWERS

Some people are passive witnesses of weird events. Others appear actively to cause them, as though they have abilities unbounded by normal rules. These people, defying logic, seem to make unbelievable things happen, sometimes for good, sometimes for sheer evil.

These are the people with strange powers.

Mother Love

In Africa, in the Far East, in Haiti, there are many stories of the evil power of voodoo. But was it voodoo that killed an American businessman in Oklahoma?

Finis P. Elton was very close to his mother. She brought him up mainly on her own, nursed him when he was sick, and always warned him to bundle up in cold weather. In the end, she loved him to death.

Finis became a successful businessman. He ran a nightclub in Ponca City, Oklahoma, which he owned in partnership with his mother. But she always dominated him, and he came to believe everything she said.

She said the nightclub was a good investment and would be a success. She was proved right.

When he fell in love and wanted to get married, she said the marriage would fail. It did fail.

Another romance went sour, as mother predicted.

Finally he met Geraldine, whom his mother did approve of. He married her, and they bought a small house in Ponca City.

Geraldine soon realized that her husband seemed to have little control over his own life. Always—before he did anything—he asked his mother's advice. It seemed almost as though he were asking her permission.

Worse, whenever he could take a weekend off work, he insisted on their going to stay with his mother. Not only was this miserable for Geraldine; it also made Finis ill. Every time they came back from the weekend visit, he had an attack of asthma—sometimes accompanied by fits and convulsions.

Matters came to a head in August, 1960. It was after one of the weekend visits. Finis was in the hospital, where he was recovering from an attack. "Sell the business," Geraldine pleaded. "Don't ask her—just tell her that you're going to do it. Then we can go far away and start again. I know we can—as long as we're on our own."

At last, like a man coming out of a dream, Finis agreed. They would move to another state and another life. As Geraldine left the hospital, he promised to call his mother and tell her of their plans.

The events that followed were pieced together by Dr. James Nathan of the Veterans Administration Hospital. He had examined Finis about 5 p.m., and found him all right. Then Finis must have phoned his mother. Her response was brutal: "I warned you before—I warn you again. Something terrible will happen to you. . . . Have I ever been wrong?"

Finis P. Elton knew his mother was always right. They found him, collapsed by the phone, gasping for breath. He died within the hour.

Dr. Nathan described it as a sophisticated version of voodoo death.

Suffering Root

G. Gatty Darling is a lawyer in South Carolina, a hard-headed man of the law and hardly the type to be influenced by anyone's evil wishes. Yet he told me he was almost destroyed by a "suffering root." He did not believe in its power, but there was no other way to explain what happened. He asked himself whether a jury in a court of law would decide that he had a root put on him. He had to conclude that they would. Maybe it was only his lack of belief that prevented the complete destruction of his family. What do you think?

South of Charleston, the islands on the South Carolina coast are notorious for the practice of root medicine. Every drugstore offers roots, black candles, dragon's blood powder, drive-away-evil floor wax, and many other potions that offer more than mere medical aid. Even hospital doctors use techniques of root medicine, since that is what their patients believe will affect them.

A particularly evil root bag might contain a Long John Conqueror root, the heart of a swallow, a pinch of graveyard dust (preferably from a murderer's grave), clippings from the intended victim's fingernails and hair, and for extra pain, a piece of the victim's underwear pierced with a pin. Such a root bag, left lying on the victim's property, would surely bring pain, suffering, and perhaps even death.

Mr. Darling had fired his black maid Lucille. She had been idle and incompetent, and after he found out that she had stolen some money, he gave her a week's notice.

When he got back from work he went into his bedroom to change, and found a little bundle of needles stuck at an angle into the middle of his pillow. There were two needles going one way and one the other, tied around with black thread.

At first he thought the bundle was left by mistake. Then he had the idea that Lucille might have put it there deliberately, hoping he would injure his face when he lay down. He put the pillow to one side, and was distracted by a call from his wife.

She had found their infant son burning hot and whimpering. It turned out he had an unusually dangerous double dose—measles and chicken pox at the same time.

The next day their elder son stopped breathing and was rushed into the hospital for emergency treatment.

His wife narrowly escaped a serious accident, and then came down with a highly unpleasant case of adult chicken pox. And Mr. Darling was suddenly overtaken by acute abdominal pain. The cause was a ruptured appendix. The doctor said he was lucky to survive.

Within two days the entire family had been struck down by life-threatening events. They appeared to be natural disasters—but were they?

A week later, the family was back to normal, more or less. He found the discarded pillow, and showed it to his daytime cook, Eliza. She gasped in horror when she saw the bundle of needles, and ran into the yard, screaming hysterically.

For this was a suffering root.

Oil from a Cadillac

Clayton McDowell is an oil diviner. He used to dowse on foot, but he gave that up after his leg was shot off in a barroom brawl. Now he walks with a wooden leg. On winter days when the mud is as soft and sticky as chocolate pie, he finds it safer to stay in the car.

So nowadays Clayton dowses from his Caddy. He drives along the back roads between the soya beans and the corn of Illinois, and when the fancy takes him, he turns into the fields. Every once in a while he'll take his rod from the back seat, and begin to dowse. His wife Marge grabs the wheel and steers between the rocks and the trees, which isn't always easy with Clayton still treading on the pedals.

Their progress would be greater if Marge could do the dowsing, but the rods won't work for her. If dowsing is a gift, then she doesn't have it.

The year I visited him outside of East Salem, Illinois, Clayton had drilled 33 wells, and found oil in 30 of them. His most spectacular find was on the land of Edwards County High School. Like most schools, it had been short of funds. Then along came Clayton and drilled a well, and the oil gushed out, making some $2,000 a day for the school. Enough to buy a whole heap of equipment.

Clayton's finds won't ever rival the big wells of Texas and Oklahoma, but they have bought his and hers Cadillacs, a fine home outside of town, and 170 trotting horses in the backyard. In their spare time, Clayton and Marge go to the trotters and to sales. Clayton told me the last horse he sold fetched $30,000. So his witching rod doesn't do too badly for him.

The rod is made of nylon, and shaped like a Y, with a tube of golden crystals at the fork. Clayton picks it up with one hand on each arm of the Y, thumbs on the inside. Then the big wrists roll until his thumbs stick straight out to right and left—until he's bent the rod from a Y almost into a T, and the tube of crystals is horizontal and pointing forward.

You need some strength to keep the slippery nylon in this position, but Clayton is used to it now. He can hold the rod horizontal halfway across Edwards County. Until, that is, he drives over some special place, where the crystals seem to twitch. The rod twists and turns in his hands, as though it were alive. The tube dips down to his knees, and the faintest suggestion of a twinkle appears in Clayton's laconic eyes. Only one thing can pull the rod down with such an irresistible force.

Black gold!

Writing from the Grave

Publishers may soon be fighting over the new Jane Austen novel, which is almost finished. Austen, one of the great writers in English literature, completed only six novels in her lifetime. The seventh is sure to create a sensation—particularly since she died in 1817.

How could she write a new novel 175 years after her death? Through the hands of retired schoolteacher Stella Horrocks, that's how. Stella's small stone house in Bradford, England, is filled with works of literature. Every table groans under the weight of exercise books crammed with writing.

According to Stella, when people die their spirits don't just evaporate. They get born again, and many get in touch with her. Her aunt Janet came through while Stella was on the train on the way home from her funeral, and other relatives have been equally quick coming back from the dead.

But it's not just family. Many creative spirits want to go on being creative, Stella explains. The great writers visit her, in spirit, and write through her hand. All she has to do is empty her mind, and her hand will start writing automatically.

Stella sits by the fireside, and appears to go into a trance. She clutches a ballpoint pen rather uncomfortably. Her fingers tighten. Suddenly her hand begins to move, apparently without any conscious thought from her. She scarcely looks at her work; her eyes are glazed. Yet the pen scurries across the book at amazing speed. Sometimes a thousand words an hour gush onto the page joined in a continuous flow.

"I couldn't possibly do all this on my own," said Stella. "I don't have the imagination. Besides, how could I use so many different kinds of handwriting?"

Austen is far from being her only author. Stella has produced a new play *Saga for an Amateur Sleuth* from Noel Coward (who died in 1973), four war stories from Somerset Maugham (died 1965), and other new works from John F. Kennedy (died 1963), Winston Churchill (died 1965), Virginia Woolf (died 1941), and even the Duke of Wellington (died 1852). Each author comes with a characteristic handwriting. "They've all different touches," adds Stella. "Noel Coward really digs into the paper, as if he was gardening."

I glanced at some of the works on display. What of the literary style? Could I recognize Jane Austen's flowery prose? Well, yes, maybe there was some similarity here, but I was surprised to find that Jane had committed a couple of grammatical errors in her first sentence. Maybe this was only because she didn't have such a good editor as I have. . . .

8. DREAMS OF DISASTER

Often when we recall dreams, they seem non-sensical, but sometimes we can recognize recent events. One theory is that dreams are the brain's way of replaying the day's happenings, in order to sift through the visual information stored in short-term memory, before discarding it.

Once in a blue moon, however, a dream may feel less like a replay, and more like a preview. This can be disturbing—even terrifying—but some dreams save lives.

Maybe some day we will learn how to control these fragments of the future.

Action Replay

David Booth was an auto mechanic in Cincinnati, Ohio. One morning in 1979 he woke sweating and crying, after a terrifying nightmare.

In it he was standing on a gravel road, with a row of trees on his left and a building on the right that might have been a school, with posters stuck in the windows. Overhead, from right to left, flew an American Airlines jet, big and silver, with three engines, one of them on the tail.

His immediate impression was that the plane was not making as much noise as he would have expected, considering how low it was.

He looked at the trees again, and at the building, and as he looked up at the plane it rolled half over, until the wings were vertical, and then plunged into the ground. There was an explosion and a fireball, and he felt death—no one on board could have survived.

His wife Pam comforted him: "David, it's only a dream!" But he could not get it out of his mind. He could not go back to sleep, and all day at work he thought about the air crash.

The next night, he had the same dream again.

He tried warm milk. He tried staying up till 2 a.m. He tried not going to sleep at all. He tried everything he could think of, but every night for eight nights he dreamed the same dream. He phoned American Airlines, but they suggested he talk to a psychiatrist.

Finally he called the Federal Aviation Administration, and spoke to officer Paul Williams. Williams took his story seriously, and on the Thursday afternoon spent 45 minutes trying to get every possible detail from Booth. Could he read the registration letters on the plane? Could he identify the building, or anything else on the ground? Booth could not produce enough information to pinpoint the location of the disaster, but he left Paul Williams with a strange foreboding.

As Williams drove home from work the following day, Friday, May 25, he heard the news of an air crash on his car radio. It was, he says, like hearing an action replay of what David Booth had told him the day before. On taking off from Chicago, American Airlines flight 191, a three-engined DC10 with one engine in the tail, had turned over and crashed into the ground, killing everyone on board.

The accident was a freak. As a result of faulty maintenance procedures, there was a failure where one engine was bolted onto the wing. As the plane reached takeoff speed, the engine came loose, swung up over the wing, and fell off behind. As it did so it sliced through all the control systems in the wing. The result was that as the plane clawed its way into the air, under a maximum load of passengers and fuel, the pilot lost not only the power from the engine but also all control over the flaps in that wing. The combined loss of power and control was what made the plane roll over and plunge into the ground.

Williams said afterwards, "It's a very unusual maneuver the plane made. Most of them crash with the wings horizontal. They run into some obstruction or there is a mid-air collision. The maneuver David described was very unusual. As a matter of fact, it's the only one I've ever heard of in a plane that size."

Fire Ahead

An hour's drive south of San Francisco through the hills, the Saratoga Convalescent Home in Quito Road housed 38 residents in February 1982, and a staff of five. The general manager of this and two other nursing homes was Frances Vernier, who lived two miles away, visiting the facility on scheduled days.

Soon after 6:30 a.m. on February 17, the residents were up and gathering for breakfast in the dining room. Dietary supervisor Anna Cabidi and her staff were cooking in the kitchen next door.

At the back of the building, next to the kitchen and dining room, was the boiler room. And in that room was a leaking gas pipe, which caught fire. By 6:40 the flames were two feet high and growing bigger.

San Jose Fire Chief Victor Marino said that if the fire had continued growing for another 15 minutes the boiler would probably have blown up, exploding through the wall into the dining room where the old folks were. It could also have devastated the kitchen. This fire was highly dangerous, and yet, because nobody lived or worked in there, the boiler room was not fitted with an automatic fire alarm. No one had any reason to go in, so the fire burned undetected.

There might easily have been a disaster, but for Frances Vernier.

Frances was not due to visit the Saratoga on that day, but in the early hours she had a dream—a nightmare that woke her up. In it, she saw patients lying in bed. She saw small flames getting progressively bigger. She saw herself running, calling to the nurses to help her get the patients out.

She dressed quickly and jumped into her car as it began to get light. Arriving at the Saratoga, she avoided her normal parking spot, leaving her car out of the way of the fire trucks that she knew would have to come. She ran directly to the door of the boiler room, opened the door a crack, and saw the flames about three feet high. The time was 6:45 a.m.

She kicked the door shut again, ran to the front, and raised the alarm. All the patients were moved to safety, and the fire was put out before the boiler blew up—so damage was slight.

There is little doubt that Frances Vernier's dream saved lives. What makes the whole thing even stranger is that she had the dream about 2:30 a.m., but—knowing that the fire would not start until it got light—she sat on her rocking chair and watched from her bedroom window until the light began to come into the sky.

Rocky, Shingly Shore

"Goddard? Didn't you hear? He's dead."

The words came as a bit of a shock. Sir Victor Goddard was at a cocktail party in Shanghai, and he spun round to see who was accusing him of being a corpse. It was a naval officer called Gladstone (who later became Admiral Sir Gerald Gladstone).

Gladstone said "I'm terribly sorry—I mean, I'm terribly glad—." When he got over his confusion, he explained that he had had a dream.

"It was so vivid I was convinced that it was actually real—that it had already happened." And he went on to say how he had seen a Dakota crashing "in a snowstorm, on a rocky, shingly shore." He had seen Goddard on board with three civilians, one of them a woman. He described the details to Sir Victor, and then they drifted apart.

Goddard wasn't worried. The weather forecast for the next day, January 14, 1946, was good. Anyway, he had no plans to take any civilian passengers. With the war over, Air Marshal Sir Victor Goddard was going home to retire. The following day, in the faithful old Dakota Sister Ann—Lord Mountbatten's personal aircraft—he was bound on the next leg of the trip, from Shanghai to Tokyo. He hoped he'd be able to fly over Hiroshima and Nagasaki, to see for himself the effects of the atom bombs.

There were just six people in the plane: Jock Campbell the pilot; two flight lieutenants; and a couple of other senior air-force officers. That didn't fit the dream, for in the dream there had been three civilians. What's more, one of them had been a woman. No—the dream was clearly nothing to worry about.

While he was having dinner with the Consul, the telephone rang. A friend of his, Seymour Berry of the *Daily Telegraph*, needed to get to Japan in a hurry, and wondered whether he might be able to scrounge a lift. Goddard was happy to oblige.

As they were headed for bed, the phone rang again. The Consul himself was asked to go to a conference in Tokyo, and to take a secretary with him. Could he please go along with Goddard, and bring Dorita?

Gradually, inevitably, the conditions of the dream were fulfilled. By the time they took off at 10 in the morning they had precisely the right combination of people on board. However, the weather was fine—the idea of a snowstorm seemed remote.

They did fly over Hiroshima, but Goddard could see nothing. To get out of clouds they had to climb above 12,000 feet, which was no fun without oxygen. While they were above the clouds, and suffering some icing, the radio stopped working. They could no longer make contact with anyone.

By the time they broke through the bottom of the clouds they were lost and in trouble. Fuel was running low. The light was failing. The weather had deteriorated into storm and snow.

Suddenly there was a shout from the cockpit. The pilot had spotted a short beach where he thought he could make an emergency landing. There were some rocks, but he hoped to be able to avoid them.

A rocky, shingly shore.

Sir Victor thought that surely his number had come up.

Luckily, he was wrong. The plane landed safely. I have a photo of it parked rather lopsided on the beach. Goddard lived to tell me the tale, but the dream had come perilously close to reality.

The Three Goats

On the night of June 1, 1976, Mary Beth Cunningham had a distressing dream. She and her husband, Larry, lived on the side of a hill just outside a small town in eastern Idaho. Larry worked on the construction of the Teton Dam, along the valley.

Their neighbor had three goats in the field next to the house, and Mary Beth had grown fond of their inquisitive and slightly bossy ways. So it was hardly surprising that the goats should figure in her dream. What was distressing was that she saw them being washed away and drowned in a great flood.

Now, floods don't happen *up* the side of a hill, and there was no water within a mile of their field. But, the dream worried her. The following night she had the same dream again. She clearly recognized the goats next door, and heard their plaintive cries as they were washed helplessly downstream.

When she had the same dream a third night running, she took action. On the morning of June 4 she went to talk to the neighbors, only to find that they had just left, taking the goats with them in a trailer. She found out later that they had taken the animals to another field that they owned, where the pasture was better, on an island in the middle of the Snake River.

On June 5 the Teton Dam collapsed. Millions of gallons of water poured through a breach caused by flood waters above. Eleven people were killed. Massive damage was done by the raging torrents of the Snake River.

The goats were never seen again.

9. FOOTPRINTS OF TOMORROW

We don't have to think about time. We know it always runs forwards. Inevitably, we get older. Inevitably, Wednesday follows Tuesday. Sadly, we can never go back to repair past mistakes.

Yet occasionally it seems that someone has a glimpse into the future. Or so they say. Perhaps they are just amazingly good at guessing. . . .?

Newsflash

Saturday morning, June 1, 1974. Lesley Brennan was at home, watching an old movie on television. Suddenly, she says, it was interrupted by a newsflash—just the word NEWSFLASH on the screen—and a man's voice.

The voice said that there had been an explosion at Flixborough. A number of people had been killed and injured, and there were some technical details. She did not pay much attention—she wanted to get back to the film she was watching—but she did note the name Flixborough, because she lived nearby, and it was local news.

At Flixborough was a large chemical plant where they made some of the main ingredients for nylon. Hundreds of people were employed in the complex. It was a major corporation in the area.

The movie finished, and around 12:15 her friend Peter East and his girlfriend came over for lunch. Lesley told them about the newsflash, and together they speculated on what had gone wrong, and what the final toll would be of injuries and deaths.

The three of them were together again when the evening news came on. Sure enough, the main story was about the disaster at Flixborough. There had been a major explosion, followed by a devastating fire. Wreckage was strewn all over the site, and the death toll was still mounting.

They were startled, though, at one point, when the broadcast said that they explosion had taken place around 5 p.m. Then they laughed; the TV people had gotten it wrong again. After all, Lesley had heard the newsflash before noon, and told friends at lunchtime.

When they saw the newspapers the next day, however, they realized that Lesley's newsflash was peculiar indeed. Because the explosion had stopped the clocks at Flixborough. They were frozen at the time of the disaster—4:53 p.m.

A Million Dollars

Jeff Randolph knew he was going to win a million.

A lawyer in San Luis Obispo, he had always been fond of gambling, and often on weekends he and his friend, a judge, would fly up to Lake Tahoe, partly for the beautiful scenery, but mainly for Caesars Palace and its enticing choices of ways to win money.

In April 1979 he noticed that Caesars' had introduced a new idea. Not far from the entrance to the main hall, twelve one-armed bandits had been linked together.

They were one-dollar machines—every pull of the handle cost a dollar—and they worked just like any other machine in the world, paying back wins of 2, 3, 5, 10, and 20 dollars for particular combinations of symbols in the window. But there was one clever difference: these machines had a cumulative jackpot.

For every dollar that was put into any one of the twelve machines, a nickel was added to the cumulative jackpot, and a big electronic sign in the middle showed how the jackpot was growing. On that April day Jeff noticed that the jackpot had climbed to about $600,000.

The higher it grew, the more people came to play the machines, and the more the jackpot accumulated. He figured that by the beginning of June it should be approaching a million dollars, and that was the moment he knew he was going to win.

Every gambler is convinced that the big win is just around the corner, but Jeff said this was different—it was more than just a hunch.

On June 3 he knew that this was the weekend, and he persuaded the judge to fly up again. On the way up in the plane he shaved for the second time that day. He had never before in his life shaved twice in one day, but, he told me later, "I wanted to look presentable and extra nice for all the pictures that were going to be taken, after I won the money."

When he reached Caesars' he checked in, went up to his room, changed, and went down to the restaurant for a leisurely dinner. He knew there was no hurry.

Then he strolled into the casino, and up to the machine with his lucky number on it. He had only about $20 in change. He fed in only a dozen or so dollars before the jackpot came up. The scoreboard said $992,018—and Caesars' rounded that up to a cool million dollars.

Jeff wasn't surprised. "I knew I was going to win," he said.

The Stabbing

Mike Veshecco, district attorney in Erie County, Pennsylvania, had a charming wife, a noisy terrier dog, a smart goatee beard, and a bunch of close friends, including John Ross, county detective.

On the evening of May 5, 1980, Mr. and Mrs. Veshecco sat at home and watched the NBC movie *Breaking Away*. When it finished, they stayed tuned for the news at 11 p.m. So, by coincidence, did Mr. and Mrs. Ross.

During the news there was a commercial break. At the beginning of it Mike and his wife saw a teaser, apparently for an item in the next segment of news. They saw something like "STABBING IN CITY" or perhaps "LOCAL MAN STABBED". Afterwards, they couldn't be sure of the exact words, but they were certain it was about a local stabbing and that the City Police were involved.

Ross and his wife said they noticed only the word "STABBING," but they also got the impression that it was a local story.

Both the DA and the county detective work closely with the police on homicides, so both Mike and John expected the phone to ring before the news bulletin was over, and gloomily anticipated a long night.

But the phones did not ring, and although they watched the rest of the news with considerable interest, there was no further mention of the stabbing.

There had been communication problems between the police and the DA's office before—so Mike made a point of getting to work early the next morning. He wanted to find out about the stabbing and to sort out the communication failure, before it got any worse.

No one in the office had seen the news of the stabbing on TV.

Later in the day, Mike called the TV station, and got the news editor to read him the script. Nothing was written there about a stabbing in the city.

Mike got on the phone. As DA, he had to deal not only with the City Police and the County Police, but also the separate police forces in the neighboring counties and cities. Mike had more than 30 police authorities on his books. But now he called the City Police, because he knew from the TV news that the murder had happened in their territory. He was right. There had been a stabbing, and they were investigating it.

But one fact made it unusual indeed. The murder had not taken place until about three o'clock in the morning. The body had not been found until 7:30 a.m. When the Vesheccos and the Rosses saw the news trailer, the victim was still alive.

The Wrong Hand

John Stone was born and raised in Poole, on the south coast of England. When he left school he joined the army, which took him to India. There he much enjoyed the exotic atmosphere, the strange food, and the mystic beliefs of the East.

On his twentieth birthday he went to a religious festival. There are many of these in India, for Hindus, Muslims, and Sikhs celebrate not only their own feast days, but one another's also. John Stone went along to one such celebration, and there a holy man offered, for one rupee, to look for the future in the palm of his hand.

"I see travel, much travel," said the fakir. "You will meet a beautiful lady, and together you will make a new life together . . ." The fortune-telling went along predictable paths, until suddenly the holy man caught his breath. ". . . And that is all I can tell you, Sahib." John was not satisfied with this sudden end, and demanded to know what else his palm foretold. At last, the Indian reluctantly said, "I regret this, Sahib, but I see death. You will die on the day you reach 40 years of age."

John felt a shiver pass through him. He paid the man, shrugged off the prophecy, and made every effort to enjoy the rest of the festival.

In due course he returned to England, got his discharge from the army, and became a truck driver. He did indeed make a new life with a beautiful lady.

But the years rolled by, and as his fortieth birthday approached, he began to worry. Surely there could be no truth in the weird prediction? And yet . . .

John told his family about the prophecy. They laughed at his fears. But as time grew short, John grew increasingly uneasy. He began calling in to say he was sick and could not drive his truck. On the actual day of his fortieth birthday he did not leave the house at all. In fact, he spent most of day in bed.

Nothing happened.

The following evening, John's father visited a club. One of the employees immediately called over to him, "Hey, Mr. Stone, I'm sorry to hear about your son."

"What about my son?"

"I heard that he died."

Three streets away, they discovered, lived another man named John Stone, born on the same day as our hero. This other John Stone had indeed died, mysteriously, on his fortieth birthday.

Could the fakir have read death in the wrong hand?

Folded Seven Times

Not long before he died I visited Rev. Donald Omand, the circus lover who became known as a chaplain to the circus. He lived in the southwest of England, and treated all circuses as his parish, circus folk as his family. He had a number of tales to tell, but none stranger than that of the old trapeze artist.

She had lived 70 years in the circus, and was treated as the head of a family of five generations of circus people.

One day she gave the reverend tea and a sealed envelope. "Please open this after I die," she said.

He assumed it was her will, and locked it safely away.

Seven years later, when she died, Donald Omand conducted the funeral service. Afterwards, he gathered the "family" around him and opened the envelope she had given him years before. To his surprise, there was no will inside—just a single piece of paper, folded seven times.

The only thing written on it was a date: the year, the month, and the day of her death.

Index